CREATING ROUTINES FOR BEGINNERS

THE ULTIMATE GUIDE TO CREATING NEW ROUTINES
ONE SMALL HABIT AT A TIME
INCLUDES 20 WEEK ROUTINE PLANNER

CONTENTS

WHAT IS A ROUTINE?

A routine is any set of actions that are repeated, habitually, and without much idea. Routines can be found in different sizes. They can be as little and easy as the few keystrokes it takes to turn on and your computer, or as big and complicated as the everyday schedule that keeps you and your household fed, cleaned, clothed, and attending your work, school, and pastime.

For most of us, our days are made up of different regimens, sewn together. We have a routine upon waking, a routine for getting to work, a regimen we do when we get to the office, a routine at the fitness center, and so on.

By their very nature, routines occur on auto-pilot, releasing our minds for other things. After all, can you keep in mind in detail precisely how you got to work this morning? Or did you just arrive somehow, without actually remembering all the actions? If you are like most people, your commute to work happens automatically. You walk to the bus or pull onto the highway while considering other things. It's precisely this automated nature of regimens that makes them powerful. Once we make something a regular routine, we no longer have to focus on it.

WHAT IS A ROUTINE?

So, the key to harnessing the power of routines is recognizing those portions of every day that have ended up being routine. The next step is to analyze those regimens. Are they helping you or harming you? Recognize what works and what does not, then alter your routine to enhance your life in whichever way you pick – whether you want to complete your book, get in shape, arrange your life, or simply have more time for your kids.

EXAMPLES OF ROUTINES THAT WORK

Numerous effective and innovative individuals have utilized the power of routine to get their work done.

THE EARLY BIRD CATCHES THE WORM

While many writers contempt the tyranny of "workplace jobs," a few of the most influential writers in the world preserve stricter schedules than the majority of bosses would ever hold them to. For example, Japanese author Haruki Murakami gets up at 4 am every day and composes for 5 or 6 hours. In the afternoon, he runs, swims, or both then reads and listens to music. He then goes to sleep every day at 9 pm. Murakami maintains this schedule for six months to a year while he is working on each book.

Much more disciplined than Murakami is American author Danielle Steele, who has composed 179 books and counting. Steele is at her typewriter every day by 8:30 am, nibbling on the very same breakfast every day: toast and a decaf iced coffee. She keeps typing for hours, declaring to work as much as 24 hr. directly when the words are streaming. Keep in mind that while this particular schedule may work well for Steele, sleep experts suggest that adults get at least seven to eight hours of sleep every night to be as healthy and efficient as possible.

MUNDANE OUTFITS, CLEVER MINDS

While numerous creative experts and business owners take wild dangers in their work, they trust in a regular routine to alleviate tension and free up mental space for more crucial decisions in their personal lives. Choosing an everyday uniform is a typical manner in which innovative individuals limit the choices they need to make each day.

Facebook creator Mark Zuckerberg is well-known for his limited wardrobe of grey t-shirt, jeans, and hoodies. While he has been seen in a suite on rare events, he primarily stays with his uniform. He declares that by constantly wearing the same thing, he reduces the variety of decisions he has to make in a day to focus on more vital matters.

While Mark Zuckerberg's closet is mainly restricted, he isn't alone in restricting his clothing choices. Designer Vera Wang, despite developing some of the most lovely and elegant bridal gown on the planet, limits her wardrobe to a handful of fundamentals, all in black. Designer Michael Kors likewise keeps to a streamlined black closet of sports jackets, t-shirt, pants, and loafers.

SiMPLE MEALS

Many people tend to consume the same breakfast and lunch day after day, however, Norwegians take "boring" meals one step further. In Norway, almost everybody brings precisely the same type of lunch to work each day, and this routine may be one reason Norway has among the highest scores for quality of life on the planet. Daily around noon, almost all Norwegians reach into their packs for their matpakke, a stack of several pieces of brown bread with a thin layer of butter and a piece of cheese, meat crown, or smoked salmon. This stack of open-faced sandwiches is wrapped in brown paper.

This basic lunch has many advantages: it can be made in a few minutes; it can be carried in a knapsack without harm or mess; it does not need refrigeration or heating, and it can be quickly eaten. This last point is crucial. In Norway, lunches last only thirty minutes. These quick lunches keep Norway's working hours amongst the fastest worldwide, an average of just 38.5 hours each week, which helps boost their quality of life.

M   **T**   **W**   **TH**   **F**   **S**   **SU**

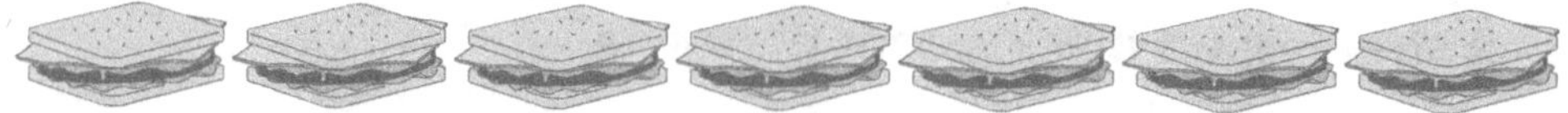

THE MANY ADVANTAGES OF FOLLOWING A ROUTINE

As the examples above show, routines can be an effective way to maximize your day. Here are some advantages of following a routine:

PREVENTING CHOICE FATIGUE

Every day, we need to make countless choices. Our brains are constantly making choices, from the small (which shirt to wear) to the huge (which business to award a contract to). Every time we contemplate the options and decide, it uses a bit of psychological energy. Our store of psychological energy is finite, and as it goes out, it becomes more and more challenging to make decisions. This can result in procrastination, snap judgments, and bad decision-making, on top of unnecessary stress.

This holds true even when we are making fun choices, such as vacation planning or choosing items for a registry. For instance, one study revealed that volunteers enjoyed choosing fantasy products for a theoretical wedding event for around 4 minutes. By minute 12, making decisions-- even enjoyable decisions-- was stressful.

Naturally, making decisions is an integral part of life. After all, making decisions is how we choose our education, jobs, and life partners. So, how can we leave needless decision-making and maintain energy for those choices that truly matter? The answer is to set a routine you don't need to think about for the simple things to save your decision-making capabilities for the important things in life.

TIME-SAVING

Have you ever lost your keys, your wallet, or your work badge? For how long did you waste looking before your items turned up?

Everyone loses something from time to time, but establishing a routine can save you time if you frequently lose essential products. Create a location for all the everyday items you need and return them to their place every day. Likewise, if you misplace crucial files at work or frequently forget products on your to-do list, developing a routine for organizing and monitoring your essential documents will save you energy and time and let you get your work done quicker.

MONEY SAVINGS

Do you eat lunch out every day? Or grab a daily latte and a muffin from the coffee bar for breakfast? The practice of eating in restaurants is a routine, and it could be costing you a great deal of cash. Instead, develop a regimen of buying groceries and prepping simple breakfasts and lunches as soon as a week. You'll save money and time in the long run.

By a similar token, establishing a consistent look can help you spend your clothing budget plan carefully and avoid impulse looking for clothing that doesn't match you or your way of life. It can likewise save time getting dressed each morning. Of course, a consistent uniform doesn't have to be all uninteresting black. Think of Angela Merkel's signature colored jackets, Diane Von Furstenberg's vibrantly printed gowns, or Kanye West's color-coordinated sweatsuits. The concept is to choose something that works for you and stick to it.

BOOSTING HEALTH

According to CDC, just 23% of Americans get the suggested amount of workout each week. Adults should perform strength training workouts two times a week and get 150 minutes of vigorous movement every week, equal to a 25-minute walk each day.

Even fewer Americans get enough fruit and vegetables every day, with just one in ten eating the suggested four to five cups of fruits and veggies per day. If you aren't the individual who awakens feeling encouraged to hit the health club and consume broccoli (and really, who is?), a routine can help.

The secret to a routine is that it does not depend upon inspiration-- you do it out of practice. If you want to get healthy, make physical fitness and healthy eating part of your routine. For instance, add a serving or two of fruit and vegetables to every meal, and when you get home from work, walk around the block a few times before you go in the door.

HELPING YOU SLEEP

Another crucial benefit of routines is their ability to help you get the sleep you require. If you struggle to get a complete 7 to eight hours of sleep each night, your pre-bed regimen could be the perpetrator. If you invest the moments before bed reading demanding news articles, responding to work e-mails, or viewing action films, it's no surprise it's hard to relax and sleep.

For the very best sleep, specialists recommend shutting off Televisions, computer systems, tablets, and phones a minimum of an hour before bedtime and developing your relaxing ritual. Whether you extend, drink warm milk, checked out a cozy book, or listen to a soothing podcast, find something that unwinds you and do it every night. Soon, your brain will recognize your bedtime routine and help you drift off faster and sleep more deeply.

SUCCESSFUL ROUTINE TIPS

TWEAKING YOUR EXISTING ROUTINES

The initial step is to determine the routines you currently have. Consider what you do when you get up and go to sleep, how you make dinner, what you do when you get to the office, and so on. Are there parts of your day that are stressful, chaotic, or take much more time than they deserve? Those are the areas where you can make improvements.

For example, if you can never discover your keys, make a routine of putting them in the exact location every day. If making dinner takes too long since your kitchen area is a catastrophe, start a routine of cleaning every evening before you turn on the TELEVISION. By making minor tweaks like these, you'll make a significant distinction in your day-to-day fulfillment.

ATTACH CHANGE TO EXISTING ROUTINES

When you want to start a brand-new routine, the most efficient strategies are to connect the routine to something you currently do habitually. For instance, if you want to begin flossing and you currently brush your teeth each night, floss every day before you brush your teeth. If you're going to start walking for 20 minutes each day and you already take the bus, begin leaving one stop early and walk the remainder of the way.

START SMALL

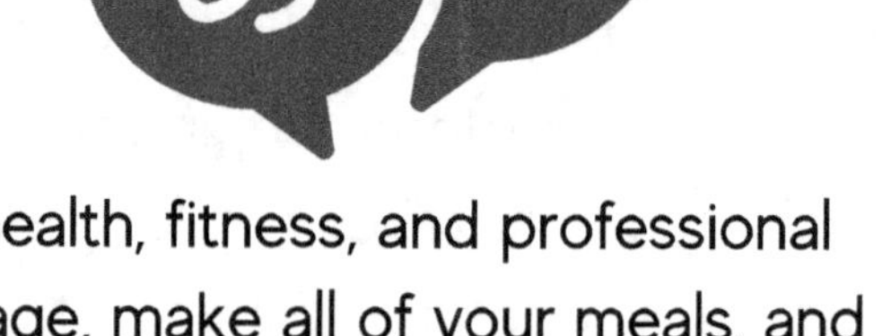

If you want to enhance your health, fitness, and professional customers, learn a new language, make all of your meals, and perhaps a few other things, do not do them simultaneously.

Make a list of everything you want to do and decide on one or two things that are most important to you. Start there. Now, consider a couple of small tweaks to your day that will get you closer to your objective. For example, if you want to get more organized, begin by cleaning for 10 minutes before consuming dessert each night. Once you have successfully made one change and stuck to it for a couple of weeks, add another modification.

PICK THE MOTIVATION THAT WORKS

There are many methods for motivating a modification in routine. For example:

- Make an X on the calendar for every day you finish your routine, and attempt to maintain your streak

- Tell a friend about your goals, and inquire about checking in regularly

- Compete with a friend to see who can stay with the goal most effectively

- Produce a sense of identity around your goal; that is, see yourself as "an individual who eats healthily" instead of thinking, "I need to consume another salad today, ugh ...".

The trick to effectively use these techniques is to acknowledge which ones work for your personality and which ones don't. For example, some people enjoy absolutely nothing more than ticking a product off a plan.

For others, a well-laid-out order of business makes them wish to run shouting in the other directions. Some individuals are very inspired when another individual holds them liable, while others are motivated by doing things differently from other people.

PICK THE MOTIVATION
THAT WORKS

When you prepare your brand-new routine, be reasonable about what motivates you, and prepare your rewards appropriately.

BE REASONABLE ABOUT HOW LONG IT REQUIRES TO FORM A HABIT.

The internet has many 21- or 30-day obstacles that pledge to kick-start a brand-new habit in merely 3 or 4 weeks. Yet, the reality is, it can take several months for a brand-new practice to end up being automated. For instance, a 2009 study of routine development found that volunteers took anywhere from 18 to 254 days to form a new practice, with the average being around 66 days.

If you are struggling because a brand-new routine does not feel like a habit yet, it helps to understand that it's normal for a habit to time to develop.

In the back of this book you will have a Habit Tracker that will help you to form habits that will sustain overtime.

GETTING BACK ON TRACK

Once you've made the effort of developing a routine, it's just going to continue forever, right? Sadly, no. No matter how well established your routine is, sometimes life occurs. You might get ill, go on vacation, have visitors, or simply get tired and neglect your routine for a few days. It doesn't matter why your routine was broken; the secret is to return to normal as soon as you can. Here are some suggestions on how:

Don't have an all-or-nothing frame of mind. Often, if we feel we need to do something every day and then miss a day, it feels like failure. Then, negative emotions can embed in, making it much harder to return to your routine. However, remember that life isn't all-or-nothing. If you miss a day of your routine, it's okay! Simply get back at it tomorrow.

Tweak your routine. In some cases, we stop following a routine since it doesn't serve us well anymore. Any time you take a break from regular, think about why. If you realize that you stopped because something wasn't working, adjust as needed and attempt again.

GETTING BACK ON TRACK

Keep in mind: in some cases, a routine is a rut. While routines use a way to get a few of life's busywork out of the way on autopilot, it is necessary not to let everything be on autopilot. If you are so entrenched in your routine that you haven't changed your hair in a decade, or you consume the very same thing for supper every single day, possibly it's time to shake things up. Modify your routine, try something new, and breathe some fresh air into your day.

A routine is any set of jobs that we perform habitually, without requiring much thought. Since it's simple to follow a routine without too much idea or tension, routines can be an effective tool for enhancing our days.

When we choose something that used to take energy – such as disputing what outfit to use or what to produce breakfast – and turn it into a regular (it's Tuesday, so I'll have oatmeal and use the navy suit), we maximize mental energy for the crucial choices in life.

By recognizing areas where your life might benefit from a routine, you can harness the power of routines to help make you more efficient and less stressed.

20 WEEK
ROUTINE PLANNER

NEW ROUTINE LIST

Make a list of everything you want to do and decide on one or two things that are most important to you. Start there.

1	
2	
3	
4	
5	
6	
7	
8	

NEW ROUTINE LIST

Now, think of one or two small tweaks to your day that will get you closer to your goal. For example, if you want to get more organized, start by tidying for 10 minutes before you eat dessert each night. Once you have successfully made one change and stuck to it for a few weeks, add another change.

GOAL:

1

NEW ROUTINE	CURRENT ROUTINE

GOAL:

2

NEW ROUTINE	CURRENT ROUTINE

NEW ROUTINE LIST

GOAL:	
3	

NEW ROUTINE	CURRENT ROUTINE

GOAL:	
4	

NEW ROUTINE	CURRENT ROUTINE

GOAL:	
5	

NEW ROUTINE	CURRENT ROUTINE

NEW ROUTINE LIST

GOAL:

6

NEW ROUTINE	CURRENT ROUTINE

GOAL:

7

NEW ROUTINE	CURRENT ROUTINE

GOAL:

8

NEW ROUTINE	CURRENT ROUTINE

1 ROUTINE

M	T	W	TH	F	S	SU

DATE:

WAKE UP TIME:

NEW ROUTINE:

GOAL:

2   ROUTINE

M	T	W	TH	F	S	SU

DATE:

WAKE UP TIME:

NEW ROUTINE:

GOAL:

3 ROUTINE

M	T	W	TH	F	S	SU

DATE:

WAKE UP TIME:

NEW ROUTINE:

GOAL:

ROUTINE

M	T	W	TH	F	S	SU

DATE:

WAKE UP TIME:

NEW ROUTINE:

GOAL:

5 ROUTINE

M	T	W	TH	F	S	SU

DATE:

WAKE UP TIME:

NEW ROUTINE:

GOAL:

ROUTINE

M	T	W	TH	F	S	SU

DATE:

WAKE UP TIME:

NEW ROUTINE:

GOAL:

7 ROUTINE

M	T	W	TH	F	S	SU

DATE:

WAKE UP TIME:

NEW ROUTINE:

GOAL:

8 ROUTINE

M	T	W	TH	F	S	SU

DATE:

WAKE UP TIME:

NEW ROUTINE:

GOAL:

SLEEP ROUTINE

For the very best sleep, specialists recommend shutting off Televisions, computer systems, tablets, and phones a minimum of an hour before bedtime and developing your relaxing ritual. Whether you extend, drink warm milk, checked out a cozy book, or listen to a soothing podcast, find something that unwinds you and do it every night. Soon, your brain will recognize your bedtime routine and help you drift off faster and sleep more deeply.

WAKE UP TiME:

NiGHTTiME ROUTiNE:

GOAL:

1
WEEK

GOALS:

1
2
3
4
5
6
7
8

MOTIVATION:

REWARD:

MEALS

WEEK OF:	BREAKFAST	LUNCH	DINNER	SNACK
M				
T				
W				
TH				
F				
S				
SU				

OUTFITS

	WORK	EXERCISE	HOME	GOING OUT
M				
T				
W				
TH				
F				
S				
SU				

DAILY ROUTINE

M	T	W	TH	F	S	SU

WAKE UP TIME:

DATE:

GOALS	ROUTINES	MEALS: ✓
1	1	B
2	2	L
3	3	
4	4	D
5	5	
6	6	S
7	7	
8	8	

MOTIVATION

GOAL ACHIEVE?	INFORMED ACCOUNTABILITY PARTNER	REWARD
Y N	Y N	

Notes:_______________________________

____

____

____

DAILY ROUTINE

M	T	W	TH	F	S	SU

WAKE UP TIME:

DATE:

MEALS: ✓

GOALS	ROUTINES	
1	1	B
2	2	L
3	3	
4	4	D
5	5	
6	6	S
7	7	
8	8	

MOTIVATION

GOAL ACHIEVE?	INFORMED ACCOUNTABILITY PARTNER	REWARD
Y N	Y N	

Notes:_______________________________________

____

____

____

DAILY ROUTINE

M	T	W	TH	F	S	SU

WAKE UP TIME:

DATE:

MEALS: ✓

GOALS	ROUTINES	
1	1	B
2	2	L
3	3	
4	4	D
5	5	
6	6	S
7	7	
8	8	

MOTIVATION

GOAL ACHIEVE?	INFORMED ACCOUNTABILITY PARTNER	REWARD
Y N	Y N	

Notes:

DAILY ROUTINE

M	T	W	TH	F	S	SU

WAKE UP TIME:

DATE:

GOALS	ROUTINES	MEALS: ✓
1	1	B
2	2	L
3	3	D
4	4	S
5	5	
6	6	
7	7	
8	8	

MOTIVATION

GOAL ACHIEVE?	INFORMED ACCOUNTABILITY PARTNER	REWARD
Y N	Y N	

Notes:____________________________________

____

____

____

DAILY ROUTINE

M	T	W	TH	F	S	SU

WAKE UP TIME:

DATE:

GOALS	ROUTINES	MEALS: ✓
1	1	B
2	2	L
3	3	D
4	4	S
5	5	
6	6	
7	7	
8	8	

MOTIVATION

GOAL ACHIEVE?	INFORMED ACCOUNTABILITY PARTNER	REWARD
Y N	Y N	

Notes:_______________________________________

____

____

____

DAILY ROUTINE

M	T	W	TH	F	S	SU

WAKE UP TIME:

DATE:

GOALS	ROUTINES	MEALS: ✓
1	1	B
2	2	L
3	3	D
4	4	S
5	5	
6	6	
7	7	
8	8	

MOTIVATION

GOAL ACHIEVE?	INFORMED ACCOUNTABILITY PARTNER	REWARD
Y N	Y N	

Notes:_______________________________________

____

____

____

DAILY ROUTINE

M	T	W	TH	F	S	SU

WAKE UP TIME:

DATE:

GOALS	ROUTINES	MEALS: ✓
1	1	B
2	2	L
3	3	D
4	4	S
5	5	
6	6	
7	7	
8	8	

MOTIVATION

GOAL ACHIEVE?	INFORMED ACCOUNTABILITY PARTNER	REWARD
Y N	Y N	

Notes:_________________________________

____

____

____

2
WEEK

GOALS:

1 ____
2 ____
3 ____
4 ____
5 ____
6 ____
7 ____
8 ____

MOTIVATION:

____

____

____

REWARD:

____

____

MEALS

WEEK OF:	BREAKFAST	LUNCH	DINNER	SNACK
M				
T				
W				
TH				
F				
S				

WEEK OF:	BREAKFAST	LUNCH	DINNER	SNACK
SU				

OUTFITS

	WORK	EXERCISE	HOME	GOING OUT
M				
T				
W				
TH				
F				
S				
SU				

DAILY ROUTINE

M	T	W	TH	F	S	SU

WAKE UP TIME:

DATE:

GOALS	ROUTINES	MEALS: ✓
1	1	B
2	2	L
3	3	
4	4	D
5	5	
6	6	S
7	7	
8	8	

MOTIVATION

GOAL ACHIEVE?	**INFORMED ACCOUNTABILITY PARTNER**	**REWARD**
Y N	Y N	

Notes:________________________________

____

____

____

DAILY ROUTINE

M	T	W	TH	F	S	SU

WAKE UP TIME:

DATE:

MEALS: ✓

GOALS	ROUTINES
1	1
2	2
3	3
4	4
5	5
6	6
7	7
8	8

B
L
D
S

MOTIVATION

GOAL ACHIEVE?	INFORMED ACCOUNTABILITY PARTNER	REWARD
Y N	Y N	

Notes:_______________________________________

____

____

____

DAILY ROUTINE

M	T	W	TH	F	S	SU

WAKE UP TIME:

DATE:

GOALS	ROUTINES	MEALS: ✓
1	1	B
2	2	L
3	3	D
4	4	S
5	5	
6	6	
7	7	
8	8	

MOTIVATION

GOAL ACHIEVE?	INFORMED ACCOUNTABILITY PARTNER	REWARD
Y N	Y N	

Notes:_______________________________

____

____

____

DAILY ROUTINE

M	T	W	TH	F	S	SU

WAKE UP TIME:

DATE:

MEALS: ✓

GOALS	ROUTINES
1	1
2	2
3	3
4	4
5	5
6	6
7	7
8	8

B
L
D
S

MOTIVATION

GOAL ACHIEVE?	INFORMED ACCOUNTABILITY PARTNER	REWARD
Y N	Y N	

Notes:_______________________________________

____

____

____

DAILY ROUTINE

M	T	W	TH	F	S	SU

WAKE UP TIME:

DATE:

GOALS	ROUTINES	MEALS: ✓
1	1	B
2	2	L
3	3	D
4	4	S
5	5	
6	6	
7	7	
8	8	

MOTIVATION

GOAL ACHIEVE?		INFORMED ACCOUNTABILITY PARTNER		REWARD
Y	N	Y	N	

Notes:________________________________

____

____

____

DAILY ROUTINE

M	T	W	TH	F	S	SU

WAKE UP TIME:

DATE:

GOALS	ROUTINES	MEALS: ✓
1	1	B
2	2	L
3	3	D
4	4	S
5	5	
6	6	
7	7	
8	8	

MOTIVATION

GOAL ACHIEVE?	INFORMED ACCOUNTABILITY PARTNER	REWARD
Y N	Y N	

Notes:_______________________________________

____

____

____

DAILY ROUTINE

M	T	W	TH	F	S	SU

WAKE UP TIME:

DATE:

GOALS		ROUTINES		MEALS: ✓
1		1		B
2		2		L
3		3		L
4		4		D
5		5		D
6		6		S
7		7		S
8		8		

MOTIVATION

GOAL ACHIEVE?		INFORMED ACCOUNTABILITY PARTNER		REWARD
Y	N	Y	N	

Notes:___________________________

____

____

____

3
WEEK

GOALS:

1
2
3
4
5
6
7
8

MOTIVATION:

REWARD:

MEALS

WEEK OF:	BREAKFAST	LUNCH	DINNER	SNACK
M				
T				
W				
TH				
F				
S				

WEEK OF:	BREAKFAST	LUNCH	DINNER	SNACK
SU				

OUTFITS

	WORK	EXERCISE	HOME	GOING OUT
M				
T				
W				
TH				
F				
S				
SU				

DAILY ROUTINE

M	T	W	TH	F	S	SU

WAKE UP TIME:

DATE:

GOALS	ROUTINES	MEALS: ✓
1	1	B
2	2	L
3	3	
4	4	D
5	5	
6	6	S
7	7	
8	8	

MOTIVATION

GOAL ACHIEVE?		INFORMED ACCOUNTABILITY PARTNER		REWARD
Y	N	Y	N	

Notes:____

____

____

____

DAILY ROUTINE

M	T	W	TH	F	S	SU

WAKE UP TIME:

DATE:

GOALS	ROUTINES	MEALS: ✓
1	1	B
2	2	L
3	3	D
4	4	S
5	5	
6	6	
7	7	
8	8	

MOTIVATION

GOAL ACHIEVE?	INFORMED ACCOUNTABILITY PARTNER	REWARD
Y N	Y N	

Notes:_______________________________

____

____

____

DAILY ROUTINE

M	T	W	TH	F	S	SU

WAKE UP TIME:

DATE:

GOALS	ROUTINES	MEALS: ✓
1	1	B
2	2	L
3	3	D
4	4	S
5	5	
6	6	
7	7	
8	8	

MOTIVATION

GOAL ACHIEVE?	INFORMED ACCOUNTABILITY PARTNER	REWARD
Y N	Y N	

Notes:_______________________________

____

____

____

DAILY ROUTINE

M	T	W	TH	F	S	SU

WAKE UP TIME:

DATE:

MEALS: ✓

GOALS	ROUTINES	
1	1	B
2	2	L
3	3	
4	4	D
5	5	
6	6	S
7	7	
8	8	

MOTIVATION

GOAL ACHIEVE?	INFORMED ACCOUNTABILITY PARTNER	REWARD
Y N	Y N	

Notes:_______________________________________

____

____

____

DAILY ROUTINE

M	T	W	TH	F	S	SU

WAKE UP TIME:

DATE:

GOALS	ROUTINES	MEALS: ✓
1	1	B
2	2	L
3	3	
4	4	D
5	5	
6	6	S
7	7	
8	8	

MOTIVATION

GOAL ACHIEVE?	INFORMED ACCOUNTABILITY PARTNER	REWARD
Y N	Y N	

Notes:_______________________________________

____

____

____

DAILY ROUTINE

M	T	W	TH	F	S	SU

WAKE UP TIME:

DATE:

GOALS	ROUTINES	MEALS: ✓
1	1	B
2	2	L
3	3	D
4	4	S
5	5	
6	6	
7	7	
8	8	

MOTIVATION

GOAL ACHIEVE?	INFORMED ACCOUNTABILITY PARTNER	REWARD
Y N	Y N	

Notes:_________________________

____

____

____

DAILY ROUTINE

M	T	W	TH	F	S	SU

WAKE UP TIME:

DATE:

GOALS	ROUTINES	MEALS: ✓
1	1	B
2	2	L
3	3	D
4	4	S
5	5	
6	6	
7	7	
8	8	

MOTIVATION

GOAL ACHIEVE?	INFORMED ACCOUNTABILITY PARTNER	REWARD
Y N	Y N	

Notes:_______________________________________
____
____
____

4
WEEK

GOALS:

1
2
3
4
5
6
7
8

MOTIVATION:

REWARD:

MEALS

WEEK OF:	BREAKFAST	LUNCH	DINNER	SNACK
M				
T				
W				
TH				
F				
S				
SU				

OUTFITS

	WORK	EXERCISE	HOME	GOING OUT
M				
T				
W				
TH				
F				
S				
SU				

DAILY ROUTINE

M	T	W	TH	F	S	SU

WAKE UP TIME:

DATE:

GOALS	ROUTINES	MEALS: ✓
1	1	B
2	2	L
3	3	
4	4	D
5	5	
6	6	S
7	7	
8	8	

MOTIVATION

GOAL ACHIEVE?	INFORMED ACCOUNTABILITY PARTNER	REWARD
Y N	Y N	

Notes:________________________________

____

____

____

DAILY ROUTINE

M	T	W	TH	F	S	SU

WAKE UP TIME:

DATE:

GOALS	ROUTINES	MEALS: ✓
1	1	B
2	2	L
3	3	D
4	4	S
5	5	
6	6	
7	7	
8	8	

MOTIVATION

GOAL ACHIEVE?	INFORMED ACCOUNTABILITY PARTNER	REWARD
Y N	Y N	

Notes:____________________________________

____

____

____

DAILY ROUTINE

M	T	W	TH	F	S	SU

WAKE UP TIME:

DATE:

GOALS	ROUTINES	MEALS: ✓
1	1	B
2	2	L
3	3	D
4	4	S
5	5	
6	6	
7	7	
8	8	

MOTIVATION

GOAL ACHIEVE?	INFORMED ACCOUNTABILITY PARTNER	REWARD
Y N	Y N	

Notes:_______________________________

____

____

____

DAILY ROUTINE

M	T	W	TH	F	S	SU

WAKE UP TIME:

DATE:

MEALS: ✓

GOALS	ROUTINES
1	1
2	2
3	3
4	4
5	5
6	6
7	7
8	8

B
L
D
S

MOTIVATION

GOAL ACHIEVE?	INFORMED ACCOUNTABILITY PARTNER	REWARD
Y N	Y N	

Notes:____

____

____

____

DAILY ROUTINE

M	T	W	TH	F	S	SU

WAKE UP TIME:

DATE:

GOALS	ROUTINES	MEALS: ✓
1	1	B
2	2	L
3	3	D
4	4	S
5	5	
6	6	
7	7	
8	8	

MOTIVATION

GOAL ACHIEVE?	INFORMED ACCOUNTABILITY PARTNER	REWARD
Y N	Y N	

Notes:_______________________________________

____

____

____

DAILY ROUTINE

M	T	W	TH	F	S	SU

WAKE UP TIME:

DATE:

GOALS	ROUTINES	MEALS: ✓
1	1	B
2	2	L
3	3	D
4	4	S
5	5	
6	6	
7	7	
8	8	

MOTIVATION

GOAL ACHIEVE?	INFORMED ACCOUNTABILITY PARTNER	REWARD
Y N	Y N	

Notes:_________________________________

____

____

____

DAILY ROUTINE

M	T	W	TH	F	S	SU

WAKE UP TIME:

DATE:

GOALS	ROUTINES	MEALS: ✓
1	1	B
2	2	L
3	3	
4	4	D
5	5	
6	6	S
7	7	
8	8	

MOTIVATION

GOAL ACHIEVE?	INFORMED ACCOUNTABILITY PARTNER	REWARD
Y　　N	Y　　N	

Notes:_______________________________________

____

____

____

5
WEEK

GOALS:

1
2
3
4
5
6
7
8

MOTIVATION:

REWARD:

MEALS

WEEK OF:	BREAKFAST	LUNCH	DINNER	SNACK
M				
T				
W				
TH				
F				
S				
SU				

OUTFITS

	WORK	EXERCISE	HOME	GOING OUT
M				
T				
W				
TH				
F				
S				
SU	WORK	EXERCISE	HOME	GOING OUT

DAILY ROUTINE

M	T	W	TH	F	S	SU

WAKE UP TIME:

DATE:

GOALS	ROUTINES	MEALS: ✓
1	1	B
2	2	L
3	3	D
4	4	S
5	5	
6	6	
7	7	
8	8	

MOTIVATION

GOAL ACHIEVE?		INFORMED ACCOUNTABILITY PARTNER		REWARD
Y	N	Y	N	

Notes:____________________________

____

____

____

DAILY ROUTINE

M	T	W	TH	F	S	SU

WAKE UP TIME:

DATE:

GOALS	ROUTINES	MEALS: ✓
1	1	B
2	2	
3	3	L
4	4	
5	5	D
6	6	
7	7	S
8	8	

MOTIVATION

GOAL ACHIEVE?	INFORMED ACCOUNTABILITY PARTNER	REWARD
Y N	Y N	

Notes:____________________________

____

____

____

DAILY ROUTINE

M	T	W	TH	F	S	SU

WAKE UP TIME:

DATE:

GOALS	ROUTINES	MEALS: ✓
1	1	B
2	2	L
3	3	D
4	4	S
5	5	
6	6	
7	7	
8	8	

MOTIVATION

GOAL ACHIEVE?	INFORMED ACCOUNTABILITY PARTNER	REWARD
Y N	Y N	

Notes:____________________________________

____

____

____

DAILY ROUTINE

M	T	W	TH	F	S	SU

WAKE UP TIME:

DATE:

GOALS	ROUTINES	MEALS: ✓
1	1	B
2	2	L
3	3	
4	4	D
5	5	
6	6	S
7	7	
8	8	

MOTIVATION

GOAL ACHIEVE?	INFORMED ACCOUNTABILITY PARTNER	REWARD
Y N	Y N	

Notes:____________________________

____

____

____

DAILY ROUTINE

M	T	W	TH	F	S	SU

WAKE UP TIME:

DATE:

GOALS	ROUTINES	MEALS: ✓
1	1	B
2	2	L
3	3	
4	4	D
5	5	
6	6	S
7	7	
8	8	

MOTIVATION

GOAL ACHIEVE?	INFORMED ACCOUNTABILITY PARTNER	REWARD
Y N	Y N	

Notes:________________________________

____

____

____

DAILY ROUTINE

M	T	W	TH	F	S	SU

WAKE UP TIME:

DATE:

GOALS	ROUTINES	MEALS: ✓
1	1	B
2	2	L
3	3	
4	4	D
5	5	
6	6	S
7	7	
8	8	

MOTIVATION

GOAL ACHIEVE?	INFORMED ACCOUNTABILITY PARTNER	REWARD
Y N	Y N	

Notes:_______________________________

____

____

____

DAILY ROUTINE

M	T	W	TH	F	S	SU

WAKE UP TIME:

DATE:

GOALS	ROUTINES	MEALS: ✓
1	1	B
2	2	L
3	3	
4	4	D
5	5	
6	6	S
7	7	
8	8	

MOTIVATION

GOAL ACHIEVE?		INFORMED ACCOUNTABILITY PARTNER		REWARD
Y	N	Y	N	

Notes:____

____

____

____

6
WEEK

GOALS:

1
2
3
4
5
6
7
8

MOTIVATION:

REWARD:

MEALS

WEEK OF:	BREAKFAST	LUNCH	DINNER	SNACK
M				
T				
W				
TH				
F				
S				
SU				

OUTFITS

	WORK	EXERCISE	HOME	GOING OUT
M				
T				
W				
TH				
F				
S				
SU				

DAILY ROUTINE

M	T	W	TH	F	S	SU

WAKE UP TIME:

DATE:

GOALS	ROUTINES	MEALS: ✓
1	1	B
2	2	L
3	3	D
4	4	S
5	5	
6	6	
7	7	
8	8	

MOTIVATION

GOAL ACHIEVE?		INFORMED ACCOUNTABILITY PARTNER		REWARD
Y	N	Y	N	

Notes:_________________________

____

____

____

DAILY ROUTINE

M	T	W	TH	F	S	SU

WAKE UP TIME:

DATE:

GOALS	ROUTINES	MEALS: ✓
1	1	B
2	2	L
3	3	D
4	4	S
5	5	
6	6	
7	7	
8	8	

MOTIVATION

GOAL ACHIEVE?	INFORMED ACCOUNTABILITY PARTNER	REWARD
Y N	Y N	

Notes:_______________________________________

____

____

____

DAILY ROUTINE

M	T	W	TH	F	S	SU

WAKE UP TIME:

DATE:

GOALS	ROUTINES	MEALS: ✓
1	1	B
2	2	L
3	3	D
4	4	S
5	5	
6	6	
7	7	
8	8	

MOTIVATION

GOAL ACHIEVE?	INFORMED ACCOUNTABILITY PARTNER	REWARD
Y N	Y N	

Notes:________________________________

____

____

____

DAILY ROUTINE

M	T	W	TH	F	S	SU

WAKE UP TIME:

DATE:

GOALS	ROUTINES	MEALS: ✓
1	1	B
2	2	L
3	3	D
4	4	S
5	5	
6	6	
7	7	
8	8	

MOTIVATION

GOAL ACHIEVE?	INFORMED ACCOUNTABILITY PARTNER	REWARD
Y N	Y N	

Notes:____________________________

____

____

____

DAILY ROUTINE

M	T	W	TH	F	S	SU

WAKE UP TIME:

DATE:

GOALS	ROUTINES	MEALS: ✓
1	1	B
2	2	L
3	3	
4	4	D
5	5	
6	6	S
7	7	
8	8	

MOTIVATION

GOAL ACHIEVE?	INFORMED ACCOUNTABILITY PARTNER	REWARD
Y N	Y N	

Notes:_______________________________

____

____

____

DAILY ROUTINE

M	T	W	TH	F	S	SU

WAKE UP TIME:

DATE:

GOALS

1
2
3
4
5
6
7
8

ROUTINES

1
2
3
4
5
6
7
8

MEALS: ✓

B

L

D

S

MOTIVATION

GOAL ACHIEVE?	INFORMED ACCOUNTABILITY PARTNER	REWARD
Y N	Y N	

Notes:______________________________________

____

____

____

DAILY ROUTINE

M	T	W	TH	F	S	SU

WAKE UP TIME:

DATE:

GOALS	ROUTINES	MEALS: ✓
1	1	B
2	2	L
3	3	
4	4	D
5	5	
6	6	S
7	7	
8	8	

MOTIVATION

GOAL ACHIEVE?		INFORMED ACCOUNTABILITY PARTNER		REWARD
Y	N	Y	N	

Notes:____

____

____

____

7
WEEK

GOALS:

1 ________________________________

2 ________________________________

3 ________________________________

4 ________________________________

5 ________________________________

6 ________________________________

7 ________________________________

8 ________________________________

MOTIVATION:

____

____

____

REWARD:

____

____

MEALS

WEEK OF:	BREAKFAST	LUNCH	DINNER	SNACK
M				
T				
W				
TH				
F				
S				
SU				

OUTFITS

	WORK	EXERCISE	HOME	GOING OUT
M				
T				
W				
TH				
F				
S				
SU				

DAILY ROUTINE

M	T	W	TH	F	S	SU

WAKE UP TIME:

DATE:

GOALS	ROUTINES	MEALS: ✓
1	1	B
2	2	L
3	3	
4	4	D
5	5	
6	6	S
7	7	
8	8	

MOTIVATION

GOAL ACHIEVE?		INFORMED ACCOUNTABILITY PARTNER		REWARD
Y	N	Y	N	

Notes:____________________________________

____

____

____

DAILY ROUTINE

M	T	W	TH	F	S	SU

WAKE UP TIME:

DATE:

MEALS: ✓

GOALS	ROUTINES	
1	1	B
2	2	L
3	3	
4	4	D
5	5	
6	6	S
7	7	
8	8	

MOTIVATION

GOAL ACHIEVE?	INFORMED ACCOUNTABILITY PARTNER	REWARD
Y N	Y N	

Notes:_______________________________________

____

____

____

DAILY ROUTINE

M	T	W	TH	F	S	SU

WAKE UP TIME:

DATE:

GOALS	ROUTINES	MEALS: ✓
1	1	B
2	2	L
3	3	D
4	4	S
5	5	
6	6	
7	7	
8	8	

MOTIVATION

	GOAL ACHIEVE?		INFORMED ACCOUNTABILITY PARTNER		REWARD
Y	N	Y	N		

Notes:_______________________________________

____

____

____

DAILY ROUTINE

M	T	W	TH	F	S	SU

WAKE UP TIME:

DATE:

GOALS	ROUTINES	MEALS: ✓
1	1	B
2	2	L
3	3	D
4	4	S
5	5	
6	6	
7	7	
8	8	

MOTIVATION

GOAL ACHIEVE?	INFORMED ACCOUNTABILITY PARTNER	REWARD
Y N	Y N	

Notes:________________________________

____

____

____

DAILY ROUTINE

M	T	W	TH	F	S	SU

WAKE UP TIME:

DATE:

MEALS: ✓

GOALS	ROUTINES
1	1
2	2
3	3
4	4
5	5
6	6
7	7
8	8

B

L

D

S

MOTIVATION

GOAL ACHIEVE?	INFORMED ACCOUNTABILITY PARTNER	REWARD
Y N	Y N	

Notes:____

____

____

____

DAILY ROUTINE

M	T	W	TH	F	S	SU

WAKE UP TIME:

DATE:

GOALS	ROUTINES	MEALS: ✓
1	1	B
2	2	L
3	3	D
4	4	S
5	5	
6	6	
7	7	
8	8	

MOTIVATION

GOAL ACHIEVE?	INFORMED ACCOUNTABILITY PARTNER	REWARD
Y N	Y N	

Notes:_______________________________

____

____

____

DAILY ROUTINE

M	T	W	TH	F	S	SU

WAKE UP TIME:

DATE:

MEALS: ✓

GOALS	ROUTINES	
1	1	B
2	2	L
3	3	
4	4	D
5	5	
6	6	S
7	7	
8	8	

MOTIVATION

GOAL ACHIEVE?		INFORMED ACCOUNTABILITY PARTNER		REWARD
Y	N	Y	N	

Notes:_______________________________________

____

____

____

8
WEEK

GOALS:

1
2
3
4
5
6
7
8

MOTIVATION:

REWARD:

MEALS

WEEK OF:	BREAKFAST	LUNCH	DINNER	SNACK
M				
T				
W				
TH				
F				
S				

WEEK OF:	BREAKFAST	LUNCH	DINNER	SNACK
SU				

OUTFITS

	WORK	EXERCISE	HOME	GOING OUT
M				
T				
W				
TH				
F				
S				
SU				

DAILY ROUTINE

M	T	W	TH	F	S	SU

WAKE UP TIME:

DATE:

GOALS	ROUTINES	MEALS: ✓
1	1	B
2	2	L
3	3	D
4	4	S
5	5	
6	6	
7	7	
8	8	

MOTIVATION

GOAL ACHIEVE?	INFORMED ACCOUNTABILITY PARTNER	REWARD
Y N	Y N	

Notes:____

____

____

____

DAILY ROUTINE

M	T	W	TH	F	S	SU

WAKE UP TIME:

DATE:

GOALS	ROUTINES	MEALS: ✓
1	1	B
2	2	L
3	3	D
4	4	S
5	5	
6	6	
7	7	
8	8	

MOTIVATION

GOAL ACHIEVE?	**INFORMED ACCOUNTABILITY PARTNER**		**REWARD**
Y N	Y	N	

Notes:_____________________________________

____

____

____

DAILY ROUTINE

M	T	W	TH	F	S	SU

WAKE UP TIME:

DATE:

GOALS	ROUTINES	MEALS: ✓
1	1	B
2	2	L
3	3	
4	4	D
5	5	
6	6	S
7	7	
8	8	

MOTIVATION

GOAL ACHIEVE?	INFORMED ACCOUNTABILITY PARTNER	REWARD
Y N	Y N	

Notes:_______________________________

____

____

____

DAILY ROUTINE

M	T	W	TH	F	S	SU

WAKE UP TIME:

DATE:

GOALS	ROUTINES	MEALS: ✓
1	1	B
2	2	L
3	3	
4	4	D
5	5	
6	6	S
7	7	
8	8	

MOTIVATION

GOAL ACHIEVE?	INFORMED ACCOUNTABILITY PARTNER	REWARD
Y N	Y N	

Notes:_________________________________

____

____

____

DAILY ROUTINE

M	T	W	TH	F	S	SU

WAKE UP TIME:

DATE:

GOALS	ROUTINES	MEALS: ✓
1	1	B
2	2	L
3	3	
4	4	D
5	5	
6	6	S
7	7	
8	8	

MOTIVATION

GOAL ACHIEVE?		INFORMED ACCOUNTABILITY PARTNER		REWARD
Y	N	Y	N	

Notes:________________________________

____

____

____

DAILY ROUTINE

M	T	W	TH	F	S	SU

WAKE UP TIME:

DATE:

MEALS: ✓

GOALS	ROUTINES	B
1	1	L
2	2	
3	3	D
4	4	
5	5	S
6	6	
7	7	
8	8	

MOTIVATION

GOAL ACHIEVE?		INFORMED ACCOUNTABILITY PARTNER		REWARD
Y	N	Y	N	

Notes:_______________________________________

____

____

____

DAILY ROUTINE

M	T	W	TH	F	S	SU

WAKE UP TIME:

DATE:

GOALS	ROUTINES	MEALS: ✓
1	1	B
2	2	L
3	3	
4	4	D
5	5	
6	6	S
7	7	
8	8	

MOTIVATION

GOAL ACHIEVE?	INFORMED ACCOUNTABILITY PARTNER	REWARD
Y N	Y N	

Notes:______________________________________

____

____

____

9
WEEK

GOALS:

1
2
3
4
5
6
7
8

MOTIVATION:

REWARD:

MEALS

WEEK OF:	BREAKFAST	LUNCH	DINNER	SNACK
M				
T				
W				
TH				
F				
S				
SU				

OUTFITS

	WORK	EXERCISE	HOME	GOING OUT
M				
T				
W				
TH				
F				
S				
SU				

DAILY ROUTINE

M	T	W	TH	F	S	SU

WAKE UP TIME:

DATE:

GOALS	ROUTINES	MEALS: ✓
1	1	B
2	2	L
3	3	D
4	4	S
5	5	
6	6	
7	7	
8	8	

MOTIVATION

GOAL ACHIEVE?		INFORMED ACCOUNTABILITY PARTNER		REWARD
Y	N	Y	N	

Notes:_________________________

____

____

____

DAILY ROUTINE

M	T	W	TH	F	S	SU

WAKE UP TIME:

DATE:

GOALS	ROUTINES	MEALS: ✓
1	1	B
2	2	L
3	3	
4	4	D
5	5	
6	6	S
7	7	
8	8	

MOTIVATION

GOAL ACHIEVE?	INFORMED ACCOUNTABILITY PARTNER	REWARD
Y N	Y N	

Notes:_______________________________________

____

____

____

DAILY ROUTINE

M	T	W	TH	F	S	SU

WAKE UP TIME:

DATE:

GOALS	ROUTINES	MEALS: ✓
1	1	B
2	2	L
3	3	
4	4	D
5	5	
6	6	S
7	7	
8	8	

MOTIVATION

GOAL ACHIEVE?		INFORMED ACCOUNTABILITY PARTNER		REWARD
Y	N	Y	N	

Notes:________________________

____

____

____

DAILY ROUTINE

M	T	W	TH	F	S	SU

WAKE UP TIME:

DATE:

GOALS	ROUTINES	MEALS: ✓
1	1	B
2	2	L
3	3	
4	4	D
5	5	
6	6	S
7	7	
8	8	

MOTIVATION

GOAL ACHIEVE?		INFORMED ACCOUNTABILITY PARTNER		REWARD
Y	N	Y	N	

Notes:____

____

____

____

DAILY ROUTINE

M	T	W	TH	F	S	SU

WAKE UP TIME:

DATE:

GOALS	ROUTINES	MEALS: ✓
1	1	B
2	2	L
3	3	
4	4	D
5	5	
6	6	S
7	7	
8	8	

MOTIVATION

GOAL ACHIEVE?		INFORMED ACCOUNTABILITY PARTNER		REWARD
Y	N	Y	N	

Notes:________________________________

____

____

____

DAILY ROUTINE

M	T	W	TH	F	S	SU

WAKE UP TIME:

DATE:

GOALS	ROUTINES	MEALS: ✓
1	1	B
2	2	L
3	3	D
4	4	S
5	5	
6	6	
7	7	
8	8	

MOTIVATION

GOAL ACHIEVE?	INFORMED ACCOUNTABILITY PARTNER	REWARD
Y N	Y N	

Notes:____

____

____

____

DAILY ROUTINE

M	T	W	TH	F	S	SU

WAKE UP TIME:

DATE:

GOALS	ROUTINES	MEALS: ✓
1	1	B
2	2	L
3	3	D
4	4	S
5	5	
6	6	
7	7	
8	8	

MOTIVATION

GOAL ACHIEVE?	INFORMED ACCOUNTABILITY PARTNER	REWARD
Y N	Y N	

Notes:_________________________

____

____

____

10
WEEK

GOALS:

1

2

3

4

5

6

7

8

MOTIVATION:

REWARD:

MEALS

WEEK OF:	BREAKFAST	LUNCH	DINNER	SNACK
M				
T				
W				
TH				
F				
S				
SU				

OUTFITS

	WORK	EXERCISE	HOME	GOING OUT
M				
T				
W				
TH				
F				
S				
SU				

DAILY ROUTINE

M	T	W	TH	F	S	SU

WAKE UP TIME:

DATE:

GOALS	ROUTINES	MEALS: ✓
1	1	B
2	2	L
3	3	
4	4	D
5	5	
6	6	S
7	7	
8	8	

MOTIVATION

GOAL ACHIEVE?	INFORMED ACCOUNTABILITY PARTNER	REWARD
Y N	Y N	

Notes:_______________________________

____

____

____

DAILY ROUTINE

M	T	W	TH	F	S	SU

WAKE UP TIME:

DATE:

GOALS	ROUTINES	MEALS: ✓
1	1	B
2	2	L
3	3	
4	4	D
5	5	
6	6	S
7	7	
8	8	

MOTIVATION

GOAL ACHIEVE?	INFORMED ACCOUNTABILITY PARTNER	REWARD
Y N	Y N	

Notes:_______________________________

____

____

____

DAILY ROUTINE

M	T	W	TH	F	S	SU

WAKE UP TIME:

DATE:

GOALS	ROUTINES	MEALS: ✓
1	1	B
2	2	L
3	3	
4	4	D
5	5	
6	6	S
7	7	
8	8	

MOTIVATION

GOAL ACHIEVE?		INFORMED ACCOUNTABILITY PARTNER		REWARD
Y	N	Y	N	

Notes:________________________________

____

____

____

DAILY ROUTINE

M	T	W	TH	F	S	SU

WAKE UP TIME:

DATE:

GOALS	ROUTINES	MEALS: ✓
1	1	B
2	2	L
3	3	
4	4	D
5	5	
6	6	S
7	7	
8	8	

MOTIVATION

GOAL ACHIEVE?	INFORMED ACCOUNTABILITY PARTNER	REWARD
Y　　　N	Y　　　N	

Notes:____________________________________

____

____

____

DAILY ROUTINE

M	T	W	TH	F	S	SU

WAKE UP TIME:

DATE:

GOALS	ROUTINES	MEALS: ✓
1	1	B
2	2	L
3	3	D
4	4	S
5	5	
6	6	
7	7	
8	8	

MOTIVATION

GOAL ACHIEVE?	INFORMED ACCOUNTABILITY PARTNER	REWARD
Y N	Y N	

Notes:_______________________________________

____

____

____

DAILY ROUTINE

M	T	W	TH	F	S	SU

WAKE UP TIME:

DATE:

GOALS	ROUTINES	MEALS: ✓
1	1	B
2	2	L
3	3	D
4	4	S
5	5	
6	6	
7	7	
8	8	

MOTIVATION

GOAL ACHIEVE?	INFORMED ACCOUNTABILITY PARTNER	REWARD
Y N	Y N	

Notes:____

____

____

____

DAILY ROUTINE

M	T	W	TH	F	S	SU

WAKE UP TIME:

DATE:

GOALS	ROUTINES	MEALS: ✓
1	1	B
2	2	L
3	3	
4	4	D
5	5	
6	6	S
7	7	
8	8	

MOTIVATION

GOAL ACHIEVE?		INFORMED ACCOUNTABILITY PARTNER		REWARD
Y	N	Y	N	

Notes:________________________________

____

____

____

11
WEEK

GOALS:

1
2
3
4
5
6
7
8

MOTIVATION:

REWARD:

MEALS

WEEK OF:	BREAKFAST	LUNCH	DINNER	SNACK
M				
T				
W				
TH				
F				
S				
SU				

OUTFITS

	WORK	EXERCISE	HOME	GOING OUT
M				
T				
W				
TH				
F				
S				
SU				

DAILY ROUTINE

M	T	W	TH	F	S	SU

WAKE UP TIME:

DATE:

GOALS	ROUTINES	MEALS: ✓
1	1	B
2	2	L
3	3	
4	4	D
5	5	
6	6	S
7	7	
8	8	

MOTIVATION

GOAL ACHIEVE?	INFORMED ACCOUNTABILITY PARTNER	REWARD
Y N	Y N	

Notes:________________________________

____

____

____

DAILY ROUTINE

M	T	W	TH	F	S	SU

WAKE UP TIME:

DATE:

GOALS	ROUTINES	MEALS: ✓
1	1	B
2	2	L
3	3	
4	4	D
5	5	
6	6	S
7	7	
8	8	

MOTIVATION

GOAL ACHIEVE?	INFORMED ACCOUNTABILITY PARTNER	REWARD
Y N	Y N	

Notes:

DAILY ROUTINE

M	T	W	TH	F	S	SU

WAKE UP TIME:

DATE:

GOALS	ROUTINES	MEALS: ✓
1	1	B
2	2	L
3	3	D
4	4	S
5	5	
6	6	
7	7	
8	8	

MOTIVATION

GOAL ACHIEVE?		INFORMED ACCOUNTABILITY PARTNER		REWARD
Y	N	Y	N	

Notes:_______________________________________

____

____

____

DAILY ROUTINE

M	T	W	TH	F	S	SU

WAKE UP TIME:

DATE:

GOALS	ROUTINES	MEALS: ✓
1	1	B
2	2	L
3	3	D
4	4	S
5	5	
6	6	
7	7	
8	8	

MOTIVATION

GOAL ACHIEVE?	INFORMED ACCOUNTABILITY PARTNER	REWARD
Y N	Y N	

Notes:________________________________

____

____

____

DAILY ROUTINE

M	T	W	TH	F	S	SU

WAKE UP TIME:

DATE:

MEALS: ✓

GOALS	ROUTINES	
1	1	B
2	2	L
3	3	
4	4	D
5	5	
6	6	S
7	7	
8	8	

MOTIVATION

GOAL ACHIEVE?	INFORMED ACCOUNTABILITY PARTNER	REWARD
Y N	Y N	

Notes:____

____

____

____

DAILY ROUTINE

M	T	W	TH	F	S	SU

WAKE UP TIME:

DATE:

GOALS	ROUTINES	MEALS: ✓
1	1	B
2	2	L
3	3	
4	4	D
5	5	
6	6	S
7	7	
8	8	

MOTIVATION

GOAL ACHIEVE?	INFORMED ACCOUNTABILITY PARTNER	REWARD
Y N	Y N	

Notes:______________________________________

____

____

____

DAILY ROUTINE

M	T	W	TH	F	S	SU

WAKE UP TIME:

DATE:

GOALS	ROUTINES	MEALS: ✓
1	1	B
2	2	L
3	3	
4	4	D
5	5	
6	6	S
7	7	
8	8	

MOTIVATION

GOAL ACHIEVE?	INFORMED ACCOUNTABILITY PARTNER	REWARD
Y N	Y N	

Notes:______________________________________

____

____

____

12 WEEK

GOALS:

1
2
3
4
5
6
7
8

MOTIVATION:

REWARD:

MEALS

WEEK OF:	BREAKFAST	LUNCH	DINNER	SNACK
M				
T				
W				
TH				
F				
S				
SU				

OUTFITS

	WORK	EXERCISE	HOME	GOING OUT
M				
T				
W				
TH				
F				
S				
SU				

DAILY ROUTINE

M	T	W	TH	F	S	SU

WAKE UP TIME:

DATE:

GOALS	ROUTINES	MEALS: ✓
1	1	B
2	2	L
3	3	D
4	4	S
5	5	
6	6	
7	7	
8	8	

MOTIVATION

GOAL ACHIEVE?	INFORMED ACCOUNTABILITY PARTNER	REWARD
Y N	Y N	

Notes:___________________________

____

____

____

DAILY ROUTINE

M	T	W	TH	F	S	SU

WAKE UP TIME:

DATE:

GOALS	ROUTINES	MEALS: ✓
1	1	B
2	2	L
3	3	
4	4	D
5	5	
6	6	S
7	7	
8	8	

MOTIVATION

GOAL ACHIEVE?	INFORMED ACCOUNTABILITY PARTNER	REWARD
Y N	Y N	

Notes:________________________________

____

____

____

DAILY ROUTINE

M	T	W	TH	F	S	SU

WAKE UP TIME:

DATE:

GOALS	ROUTINES	MEALS: ✓
1	1	B
2	2	L
3	3	
4	4	D
5	5	
6	6	S
7	7	
8	8	

MOTIVATION

GOAL ACHIEVE?	INFORMED ACCOUNTABILITY PARTNER	REWARD
Y N	Y N	

Notes:________________________________

____

____

____

DAILY ROUTINE

M	T	W	TH	F	S	SU

WAKE UP TIME:

DATE:

GOALS	ROUTINES	MEALS: ✓
1	1	B
2	2	L
3	3	D
4	4	S
5	5	
6	6	
7	7	
8	8	

MOTIVATION

GOAL ACHIEVE?	INFORMED ACCOUNTABILITY PARTNER	REWARD
Y N	Y N	

Notes:________________________________

____

____

____

DAILY ROUTINE

M	T	W	TH	F	S	SU

WAKE UP TIME:

DATE:

GOALS	ROUTINES	MEALS: ✓
1	1	B
2	2	L
3	3	D
4	4	S
5	5	
6	6	
7	7	
8	8	

MOTIVATION

GOAL ACHIEVE?	INFORMED ACCOUNTABILITY PARTNER	REWARD
Y N	Y N	

Notes:_______________________________________

____

____

____

DAILY ROUTINE

M	T	W	TH	F	S	SU

WAKE UP TIME:

DATE:

GOALS	ROUTINES	MEALS: ✓
1	1	B
2	2	L
3	3	
4	4	D
5	5	
6	6	S
7	7	
8	8	

MOTIVATION

GOAL ACHIEVE?	INFORMED ACCOUNTABILITY PARTNER	REWARD
Y N	Y N	

Notes:____________________________________

____

____

____

DAILY ROUTINE

M	T	W	TH	F	S	SU

WAKE UP TIME:

DATE:

GOALS	ROUTINES	MEALS: ✓
1	1	B
2	2	L
3	3	
4	4	D
5	5	
6	6	S
7	7	
8	8	

MOTIVATION

GOAL ACHiEVE?	INFORMED ACCOUNTABiLiTY PARTNER	REWARD
Y N	Y N	

Notes:____

____

____

____

13
WEEK

GOALS:

1
2
3
4
5
6
7
8

MOTIVATION:

REWARD:

MEALS

WEEK OF:	BREAKFAST	LUNCH	DINNER	SNACK
M				
T				
W				
TH				
F				
S				
SU				

OUTFITS

	WORK	EXERCISE	HOME	GOING OUT
M				
T				
W				
TH				
F				
S				
SU				

DAILY ROUTINE

M	T	W	TH	F	S	SU

WAKE UP TIME:

DATE:

GOALS	ROUTINES	MEALS: ✓
1	1	B
2	2	L
3	3	D
4	4	S
5	5	
6	6	
7	7	
8	8	

MOTIVATION

GOAL ACHIEVE?	INFORMED ACCOUNTABILITY PARTNER	REWARD
Y N	Y N	

Notes:_______________________________________

____

____

____

DAILY ROUTINE

M	T	W	TH	F	S	SU

WAKE UP TIME:

DATE:

GOALS	ROUTINES	MEALS: ✓
1	1	B
2	2	L
3	3	
4	4	D
5	5	
6	6	S
7	7	
8	8	

MOTIVATION

GOAL ACHIEVE?	INFORMED ACCOUNTABILITY PARTNER	REWARD
Y N	Y N	

Notes:

DAILY ROUTINE

M	T	W	TH	F	S	SU

WAKE UP TIME:

DATE:

GOALS	ROUTINES	MEALS: ✓
1	1	B
2	2	L
3	3	D
4	4	S
5	5	
6	6	
7	7	
8	8	

MOTIVATION

GOAL ACHIEVE?		INFORMED ACCOUNTABILITY PARTNER		REWARD
Y	N	Y	N	

Notes:_______________________________________

____

____

____

DAILY ROUTINE

M	T	W	TH	F	S	SU

WAKE UP TIME:

DATE:

GOALS	ROUTINES	MEALS: ✓
1	1	B
2	2	L
3	3	
4	4	D
5	5	
6	6	S
7	7	
8	8	

MOTIVATION

GOAL ACHIEVE?	INFORMED ACCOUNTABILITY PARTNER	REWARD
Y N	Y N	

Notes:____________________________________

____

____

____

DAILY ROUTINE

M	T	W	TH	F	S	SU

WAKE UP TIME:

DATE:

GOALS	ROUTINES	MEALS: ✓
1	1	B
2	2	L
3	3	
4	4	D
5	5	
6	6	S
7	7	
8	8	

MOTIVATION

GOAL ACHIEVE?	INFORMED ACCOUNTABILITY PARTNER	REWARD
Y N	Y N	

Notes:_______________________________

____

____

____

DAILY ROUTINE

M	T	W	TH	F	S	SU

WAKE UP TIME:

DATE:

GOALS	ROUTINES	MEALS: ✓
1	1	B
2	2	L
3	3	
4	4	D
5	5	
6	6	S
7	7	
8	8	

MOTIVATION

GOAL ACHIEVE?		INFORMED ACCOUNTABILITY PARTNER		REWARD
Y	N	Y	N	

Notes:___________________________

____

____

____

DAILY ROUTINE

M	T	W	TH	F	S	SU

WAKE UP TIME:

DATE:

GOALS	ROUTINES	MEALS: ✓
1	1	B
2	2	L
3	3	D
4	4	S
5	5	
6	6	
7	7	
8	8	

MOTIVATION

GOAL ACHIEVE?	INFORMED ACCOUNTABILITY PARTNER	REWARD
Y N	Y N	

Notes:____

____

____

____

14
WEEK

GOALS:

1 ____
2 ____
3 ____
4 ____
5 ____
6 ____
7 ____
8 ____

MOTIVATION:

____
____
____
____

REWARD:

____
____

MEALS

WEEK OF:	BREAKFAST	LUNCH	DINNER	SNACK
M				
T				
W				
TH				
F				
S				

WEEK OF:	BREAKFAST	LUNCH	DINNER	SNACK
SU				

OUTFITS

	WORK	EXERCISE	HOME	GOING OUT
M				
T				
W				
TH				
F				
S				
SU				

DAILY ROUTINE

M	T	W	TH	F	S	SU

WAKE UP TIME:

DATE:

GOALS	ROUTINES	MEALS: ✓
1	1	B
2	2	L
3	3	
4	4	D
5	5	
6	6	S
7	7	
8	8	

MOTIVATION

GOAL ACHiEVE?		INFORMED ACCOUNTABiLiTY PARTNER		REWARD
Y	N	Y	N	

Notes:

DAILY ROUTINE

M	T	W	TH	F	S	SU

WAKE UP TIME:

DATE:

GOALS	ROUTINES	MEALS: ✓
1	1	B
2	2	L
3	3	D
4	4	S
5	5	
6	6	
7	7	
8	8	

MOTIVATION

GOAL ACHIEVE?	INFORMED ACCOUNTABILITY PARTNER	REWARD
Y N	Y N	

Notes:______________________________

____

____

____

DAILY ROUTINE

M	T	W	TH	F	S	SU

WAKE UP TIME:

DATE:

GOALS	ROUTINES	MEALS: ✓
1	1	B
2	2	L
3	3	D
4	4	S
5	5	
6	6	
7	7	
8	8	

MOTIVATION

GOAL ACHIEVE?		INFORMED ACCOUNTABILITY PARTNER		REWARD
Y	N	Y	N	

Notes:_______________________________________

____

____

____

DAILY ROUTINE

M	T	W	TH	F	S	SU

WAKE UP TIME:

DATE:

MEALS: ✓

GOALS	ROUTINES
1	1
2	2
3	3
4	4
5	5
6	6
7	7
8	8

- B
- L
- D
- S

MOTIVATION

GOAL ACHIEVE?	INFORMED ACCOUNTABILITY PARTNER	REWARD
Y N	Y N	

Notes:_______________________________________

____

____

____

DAILY ROUTINE

M	T	W	TH	F	S	SU

WAKE UP TIME:

DATE:

GOALS	ROUTINES	MEALS: ✓
1	1	B
2	2	L
3	3	D
4	4	S
5	5	
6	6	
7	7	
8	8	

MOTIVATION

GOAL ACHIEVE?		INFORMED ACCOUNTABILITY PARTNER		REWARD
Y	N	Y	N	

Notes:________________________________

____

____

____

DAILY ROUTINE

M	T	W	TH	F	S	SU

WAKE UP TIME:

DATE:

GOALS	ROUTINES	MEALS: ✓
1	1	B
2	2	L
3	3	
4	4	D
5	5	
6	6	S
7	7	
8	8	

MOTIVATION

GOAL ACHIEVE?	INFORMED ACCOUNTABILITY PARTNER	REWARD
Y N	Y N	

Notes:____

____

____

____

DAILY ROUTINE

M	T	W	TH	F	S	SU

WAKE UP TIME:

DATE:

GOALS

1	
2	
3	
4	
5	
6	
7	
8	

ROUTINES

1	
2	
3	
4	
5	
6	
7	
8	

MEALS: ✓

- B
- L
- D
- S

MOTIVATION

GOAL ACHIEVE?		INFORMED ACCOUNTABILITY PARTNER		REWARD
Y	N	Y	N	

Notes:_______________________________

____

____

____

15
WEEK

GOALS:

1
2
3
4
5
6
7
8

MOTIVATION:

REWARD:

MEALS

WEEK OF:	BREAKFAST	LUNCH	DINNER	SNACK
M				
T				
W				
TH				
F				
S				
SU				

OUTFITS

	WORK	EXERCISE	HOME	GOING OUT
M				
T				
W				
TH				
F				
S				
SU				

DAILY ROUTINE

M	T	W	TH	F	S	SU

WAKE UP TIME:

DATE:

GOALS	ROUTINES	MEALS: ✓
1	1	B
2	2	L
3	3	D
4	4	S
5	5	
6	6	
7	7	
8	8	

MOTIVATION

GOAL ACHIEVE?	INFORMED ACCOUNTABILITY PARTNER	REWARD
Y N	Y N	

Notes:_______________________________________

____

____

____

DAILY ROUTINE

M	T	W	TH	F	S	SU

WAKE UP TIME:

DATE:

GOALS	ROUTINES	MEALS: ✓
1	1	B
2	2	L
3	3	D
4	4	S
5	5	
6	6	
7	7	
8	8	

MOTIVATION

GOAL ACHIEVE?	INFORMED ACCOUNTABILITY PARTNER	REWARD
Y N	Y N	

Notes: ______________________________________

____

____

____

DAILY ROUTINE

M	T	W	TH	F	S	SU

WAKE UP TIME:

DATE:

GOALS	ROUTINES	MEALS: ✓
1	1	B
2	2	L
3	3	
4	4	D
5	5	
6	6	S
7	7	
8	8	

MOTIVATION

GOAL ACHIEVE?	INFORMED ACCOUNTABILITY PARTNER	REWARD
Y N	Y N	

Notes:____________________________________

____

____

____

DAILY ROUTINE

M	T	W	TH	F	S	SU

WAKE UP TIME:

DATE:

GOALS	ROUTINES	MEALS: ✓

GOALS	ROUTINES
1	1
2	2
3	3
4	4
5	5
6	6
7	7
8	8

MEALS: ✓
- B
- L
- D
- S

MOTIVATION

GOAL ACHIEVE?	INFORMED ACCOUNTABILITY PARTNER	REWARD
Y　　N	Y　　N	

Notes:_______________________________________

____

____

____

DAILY ROUTINE

M	T	W	TH	F	S	SU

WAKE UP TIME:

DATE:

GOALS	ROUTINES	MEALS: ✓
1	1	B
2	2	L
3	3	D
4	4	S
5	5	
6	6	
7	7	
8	8	

MOTIVATION

GOAL ACHIEVE?	**INFORMED ACCOUNTABILITY PARTNER**	**REWARD**
Y | N	Y | N	

Notes:________________________________

____

____

____

DAILY ROUTINE

M	T	W	TH	F	S	SU

WAKE UP TIME:

DATE:

GOALS		ROUTINES		MEALS: ✓
1		1		B
2		2		L
3		3		D
4		4		S
5		5		
6		6		
7		7		
8		8		

MOTIVATION

GOAL ACHIEVE?		INFORMED ACCOUNTABILITY PARTNER		REWARD
Y	N	Y	N	

Notes:_______________________________________

____

____

____

DAILY ROUTINE

M	T	W	TH	F	S	SU

WAKE UP TIME:

DATE:

GOALS	ROUTINES	MEALS: ✓
1	1	B
2	2	L
3	3	D
4	4	S
5	5	
6	6	
7	7	
8	8	

MOTIVATION

GOAL ACHIEVE?	INFORMED ACCOUNTABILITY PARTNER	REWARD
Y	N	Y	N	

Notes:_______________________________________

____

____

____

16
WEEK

GOALS:

1 _______________________________________

2 _______________________________________

3 _______________________________________

4 _______________________________________

5 _______________________________________

6 _______________________________________

7 _______________________________________

8 _______________________________________

MOTIVATION:

____

____

____

____

REWARD:

____

____

MEALS

WEEK OF:	BREAKFAST	LUNCH	DINNER	SNACK
M				
T				
W				
TH				
F				
S				
SU				

OUTFITS

	WORK	EXERCISE	HOME	GOING OUT
M				
T				
W				
TH				
F				
S				
SU				

DAILY ROUTINE

M	T	W	TH	F	S	SU

WAKE UP TIME:

DATE:

GOALS	ROUTINES	MEALS: ✓
1	1	B
2	2	L
3	3	
4	4	D
5	5	
6	6	S
7	7	
8	8	

MOTIVATION

GOAL ACHIEVE?	INFORMED ACCOUNTABILITY PARTNER	REWARD
Y N	Y N	

Notes:____

____

____

____

DAILY ROUTINE

M	T	W	TH	F	S	SU

WAKE UP TIME:

DATE:

MEALS: ✓

GOALS	ROUTINES	
1	1	B
2	2	L
3	3	D
4	4	S
5	5	
6	6	
7	7	
8	8	

MOTIVATION

GOAL ACHIEVE?	INFORMED ACCOUNTABILITY PARTNER	REWARD
Y N	Y N	

Notes: ___________________________________

____

____

____

DAILY ROUTINE

M	T	W	TH	F	S	SU

WAKE UP TIME:

DATE:

GOALS	ROUTINES	MEALS: ✓
1	1	B
2	2	L
3	3	D
4	4	S
5	5	
6	6	
7	7	
8	8	

MOTIVATION

GOAL ACHIEVE?		INFORMED ACCOUNTABILITY PARTNER		REWARD
Y	N	Y	N	

Notes:____________________________________

____

____

____

DAILY ROUTINE

M	T	W	TH	F	S	SU

WAKE UP TIME:

DATE:

MEALS: ✓

GOALS	ROUTINES
1	1
2	2
3	3
4	4
5	5
6	6
7	7
8	8

B
L
D
S

MOTIVATION

GOAL ACHIEVE?	INFORMED ACCOUNTABILITY PARTNER	REWARD
Y N	Y N	

Notes: ________________________________

____

____

____

DAILY ROUTINE

M	T	W	TH	F	S	SU

WAKE UP TIME:

DATE:

GOALS	ROUTINES	MEALS: ✓
1	1	B
2	2	L
3	3	D
4	4	S
5	5	
6	6	
7	7	
8	8	

MOTIVATION

GOAL ACHIEVE?	INFORMED ACCOUNTABILITY PARTNER	REWARD
Y N	Y N	

Notes:_______________________________

____

____

____

DAILY ROUTINE

M	T	W	TH	F	S	SU

WAKE UP TIME:

DATE:

GOALS		ROUTINES		MEALS: ✓
1		1		B
2		2		L
3		3		D
4		4		S
5		5		
6		6		
7		7		
8		8		

MOTIVATION

GOAL ACHIEVE?		INFORMED ACCOUNTABILITY PARTNER		REWARD
Y	N	Y	N	

Notes:_______________________________________

____

____

____

DAILY ROUTINE

M	T	W	TH	F	S	SU

WAKE UP TIME:

DATE:

MEALS: ✓

GOALS	ROUTINES	
1	1	B
2	2	L
3	3	D
4	4	S
5	5	
6	6	
7	7	
8	8	

MOTIVATION

GOAL ACHIEVE?	INFORMED ACCOUNTABILITY PARTNER	REWARD
Y N	Y N	

Notes:_______________________________________

____

____

____

17
WEEK

GOALS:

1

2

3

4

5

6

7

8

MOTIVATION:

REWARD:

MEALS

WEEK OF:	BREAKFAST	LUNCH	DINNER	SNACK
M				
T				
W				
TH				
F				
S				
SU				

OUTFITS

	WORK	EXERCISE	HOME	GOING OUT
M				
T				
W				
TH				
F				
S				
SU				

DAILY ROUTINE

M	T	W	TH	F	S	SU

WAKE UP TIME:

DATE:

GOALS	ROUTINES	MEALS: ✓
1	1	B
2	2	L
3	3	
4	4	D
5	5	
6	6	S
7	7	
8	8	

MOTIVATION

GOAL ACHIEVE?		INFORMED ACCOUNTABILITY PARTNER		REWARD
Y	N	Y	N	

Notes:____

____

____

____

DAILY ROUTINE

M	T	W	TH	F	S	SU

WAKE UP TIME:

DATE:

GOALS	ROUTINES	MEALS: ✓
1	1	B
2	2	L
3	3	
4	4	D
5	5	
6	6	S
7	7	
8	8	

MOTIVATION

GOAL ACHIEVE?		INFORMED ACCOUNTABILITY PARTNER		REWARD
Y	N	Y	N	

Notes:____

____

____

____

DAILY ROUTINE

M	T	W	TH	F	S	SU

WAKE UP TIME:

DATE:

GOALS	ROUTINES	MEALS: ✓
1	1	B
2	2	L
3	3	D
4	4	S
5	5	
6	6	
7	7	
8	8	

MOTIVATION

GOAL ACHIEVE?	INFORMED ACCOUNTABILITY PARTNER	REWARD
Y N	Y N	

Notes:___________________________________

____

____

____

DAILY ROUTINE

M	T	W	TH	F	S	SU

WAKE UP TIME:

DATE:

GOALS	ROUTINES	MEALS: ✓
1	1	B
2	2	L
3	3	
4	4	D
5	5	
6	6	S
7	7	
8	8	

MOTIVATION

GOAL ACHIEVE?	INFORMED ACCOUNTABILITY PARTNER	REWARD
Y N	Y N	

Notes:________________________________

____

____

____

DAILY ROUTINE

M	T	W	TH	F	S	SU

WAKE UP TIME:

DATE:

MEALS: ✓

GOALS	ROUTINES
1	1
2	2
3	3
4	4
5	5
6	6
7	7
8	8

Meals:
- B
- L
- D
- S

MOTIVATION

GOAL ACHIEVE?	INFORMED ACCOUNTABILITY PARTNER	REWARD
Y N	Y N	

Notes:____________________________________

____

____

____

DAILY ROUTINE

M	T	W	TH	F	S	SU

WAKE UP TIME:

DATE:

GOALS	ROUTINES	MEALS: ✓
1	1	B
2	2	L
3	3	D
4	4	S
5	5	
6	6	
7	7	
8	8	

MOTIVATION

GOAL ACHIEVE?	INFORMED ACCOUNTABILITY PARTNER	REWARD
Y N	Y N	

Notes:______________________________________

____

____

____

DAILY ROUTINE

M	T	W	TH	F	S	SU

WAKE UP TIME:

DATE:

GOALS	ROUTINES	MEALS: ✓
1	1	B
2	2	L
3	3	
4	4	D
5	5	
6	6	S
7	7	
8	8	

MOTIVATION

GOAL ACHIEVE?		INFORMED ACCOUNTABILITY PARTNER		REWARD
Y	N	Y	N	

Notes:____

____

____

____

18
WEEK

GOALS:

1
2
3
4
5
6
7
8

MOTIVATION:

REWARD:

MEALS

WEEK OF:	BREAKFAST	LUNCH	DINNER	SNACK
M				
T				
W				
TH				
F				
S				

WEEK OF:	BREAKFAST	LUNCH	DINNER	SNACK
SU				

OUTFITS

	WORK	EXERCISE	HOME	GOING OUT
M				
T				
W				
TH				
F				
S				
SU				

DAILY ROUTINE

M	T	W	TH	F	S	SU

WAKE UP TIME:

DATE:

GOALS	ROUTINES	MEALS: ✓
1	1	B
2	2	L
3	3	D
4	4	S
5	5	
6	6	
7	7	
8	8	

MOTIVATION

GOAL ACHIEVE?		INFORMED ACCOUNTABILITY PARTNER		REWARD
Y	N	Y	N	

Notes:_______________________________________

____

____

____

DAILY ROUTINE

M	T	W	TH	F	S	SU

WAKE UP TIME:

DATE:

GOALS	ROUTINES	MEALS: ✓
1	1	B
2	2	L
3	3	
4	4	D
5	5	
6	6	S
7	7	
8	8	

MOTIVATION

GOAL ACHIEVE?	INFORMED ACCOUNTABILITY PARTNER	REWARD
Y N	Y N	

Notes:_______________________________________

____

____

____

DAILY ROUTINE

M	T	W	TH	F	S	SU

WAKE UP TIME:

DATE:

GOALS	ROUTINES	MEALS: ✓
1	1	B
2	2	L
3	3	
4	4	D
5	5	
6	6	S
7	7	
8	8	

MOTIVATION

GOAL ACHiEVE?		INFORMED ACCOUNTABiLiTY PARTNER		REWARD
Y	N	Y	N	

Notes:____________________________________

____

____

____

DAILY ROUTINE

M	T	W	TH	F	S	SU

WAKE UP TIME:

DATE:

GOALS	ROUTINES	MEALS: ✓
1	1	B
2	2	L
3	3	D
4	4	S
5	5	
6	6	
7	7	
8	8	

MOTIVATION

GOAL ACHIEVE?	INFORMED ACCOUNTABILITY PARTNER	REWARD
Y N	Y N	

Notes:____________________________________

____

____

____

DAILY ROUTINE

M	T	W	TH	F	S	SU

WAKE UP TIME:

DATE:

GOALS	ROUTINES	MEALS: ✓
1	1	B
2	2	L
3	3	
4	4	D
5	5	
6	6	S
7	7	
8	8	

MOTIVATION

GOAL ACHIEVE?		INFORMED ACCOUNTABILITY PARTNER		REWARD
Y	N	Y	N	

Notes:_______________________________________

____

____

____

DAILY ROUTINE

M	T	W	TH	F	S	SU

WAKE UP TIME:

DATE:

GOALS	ROUTINES	MEALS: ✓
1	1	B
2	2	L
3	3	D
4	4	S
5	5	
6	6	
7	7	
8	8	

MOTIVATION

GOAL ACHIEVE?	INFORMED ACCOUNTABILITY PARTNER	REWARD
Y N	Y N	

Notes:_______________________________________

____

____

____

DAILY ROUTINE

M	T	W	TH	F	S	SU

WAKE UP TIME:

DATE:

GOALS	ROUTINES	MEALS: ✓
1	1	B
2	2	L
3	3	D
4	4	S
5	5	
6	6	
7	7	
8	8	

MOTIVATION

GOAL ACHIEVE?	INFORMED ACCOUNTABILITY PARTNER	REWARD
Y N	Y N	

Notes:________________________________

____

____

____

19
WEEK

GOALS:

1
2
3
4
5
6
7
8

MOTIVATION:

REWARD:

MEALS

WEEK OF:	BREAKFAST	LUNCH	DINNER	SNACK
M				
T				
W				
TH				
F				
S				
SU				

OUTFITS

	WORK	EXERCISE	HOME	GOING OUT
M				
T				
W				
TH				
F				
S				
SU				

DAILY ROUTINE

M	T	W	TH	F	S	SU

WAKE UP TIME:

DATE:

GOALS	ROUTINES	MEALS: ✓
1	1	B
2	2	L
3	3	D
4	4	S
5	5	
6	6	
7	7	
8	8	

MOTIVATION

GOAL ACHIEVE?	INFORMED ACCOUNTABILITY PARTNER	REWARD
Y N	Y N	

Notes:____________________________

____

____

____

DAILY ROUTINE

M	T	W	TH	F	S	SU

WAKE UP TIME:

DATE:

GOALS	ROUTINES	MEALS: ✓
1	1	B
2	2	L
3	3	D
4	4	S
5	5	
6	6	
7	7	
8	8	

MOTIVATION

GOAL ACHIEVE?	INFORMED ACCOUNTABILITY PARTNER	REWARD
Y N	Y N	

Notes:____________________________________

____

____

____

DAILY ROUTINE

M	T	W	TH	F	S	SU

WAKE UP TIME:

DATE:

GOALS	ROUTINES	MEALS: ✓
1	1	B
2	2	L
3	3	
4	4	D
5	5	
6	6	S
7	7	
8	8	

MOTIVATION

GOAL ACHIEVE?	INFORMED ACCOUNTABILITY PARTNER	REWARD
Y N	Y N	

Notes:_______________________________________

____

____

____

DAILY ROUTINE

M	T	W	TH	F	S	SU

WAKE UP TIME:

DATE:

GOALS	ROUTINES	MEALS: ✓
1	1	B
2	2	L
3	3	
4	4	D
5	5	
6	6	S
7	7	
8	8	

MOTIVATION

GOAL ACHIEVE?		INFORMED ACCOUNTABILITY PARTNER		REWARD
Y	N	Y	N	

Notes:____________________________________

____

____

____

DAILY ROUTINE

M	T	W	TH	F	S	SU

WAKE UP TIME:

DATE:

GOALS	ROUTINES	MEALS: ✓
1	1	B
2	2	L
3	3	
4	4	D
5	5	
6	6	S
7	7	
8	8	

MOTIVATION

GOAL ACHIEVE?	INFORMED ACCOUNTABILITY PARTNER	REWARD
Y N	Y N	

Notes:_________________________

____

____

____

DAILY ROUTINE

M	T	W	TH	F	S	SU

WAKE UP TIME:

DATE:

GOALS	ROUTINES	MEALS: ✓
1	1	B
2	2	L
3	3	D
4	4	S
5	5	
6	6	
7	7	
8	8	

MOTIVATION

GOAL ACHIEVE?	INFORMED ACCOUNTABILITY PARTNER	REWARD
Y N	Y N	

Notes:_______________________________________

____

____

____

DAILY ROUTINE

M	T	W	TH	F	S	SU

WAKE UP TIME:

DATE:

GOALS	ROUTINES	MEALS: ✓
1	1	B
2	2	L
3	3	D
4	4	S
5	5	
6	6	
7	7	
8	8	

MOTIVATION

GOAL ACHIEVE?	INFORMED ACCOUNTABILITY PARTNER	REWARD
Y N	Y N	

Notes:____________________________________

____

____

____

20
WEEK

GOALS:

1
2
3
4
5
6
7
8

MOTIVATION:

REWARD:

MEALS

WEEK OF:	BREAKFAST	LUNCH	DINNER	SNACK
M				
T				
W				
TH				
F				
S				
SU				

OUTFITS

	WORK	EXERCISE	HOME	GOING OUT
M				
T				
W				
TH				
F				
S				
SU				

DAILY ROUTINE

M	T	W	TH	F	S	SU

WAKE UP TIME:

DATE:

GOALS	ROUTINES	MEALS: ✓
1	1	B
2	2	L
3	3	
4	4	D
5	5	
6	6	S
7	7	
8	8	

MOTIVATION

GOAL ACHIEVE?	INFORMED ACCOUNTABILITY PARTNER	REWARD
Y N	Y N	

Notes:_______________________________________

____

____

____

DAILY ROUTINE

M	T	W	TH	F	S	SU

WAKE UP TIME:

DATE:

GOALS	ROUTINES	MEALS: ✓
1	1	B
2	2	L
3	3	D
4	4	S
5	5	
6	6	
7	7	
8	8	

MOTIVATION

GOAL ACHIEVE?	**INFORMED ACCOUNTABILITY PARTNER**	**REWARD**
Y N	Y N	

Notes:_______________________________

____

____

____

DAILY ROUTINE

M	T	W	TH	F	S	SU

WAKE UP TIME:

DATE:

GOALS	ROUTINES	MEALS: ✓
1	1	B
2	2	L
3	3	D
4	4	S
5	5	
6	6	
7	7	
8	8	

MOTIVATION

GOAL ACHIEVE?	INFORMED ACCOUNTABILITY PARTNER	REWARD
Y N	Y N	

Notes:_______________________________________

____

____

____

DAILY ROUTINE

M	T	W	TH	F	S	SU

WAKE UP TIME:

DATE:

GOALS	ROUTINES	MEALS: ✓
1	1	B
2	2	L
3	3	
4	4	D
5	5	
6	6	S
7	7	
8	8	

MOTIVATION

GOAL ACHIEVE?	INFORMED ACCOUNTABILITY PARTNER	REWARD
Y N	Y N	

Notes:______________________________________

____

____

____

DAILY ROUTINE

M	T	W	TH	F	S	SU

WAKE UP TIME:

DATE:

GOALS	ROUTINES	MEALS: ✓
1	1	B
2	2	L
3	3	D
4	4	S
5	5	
6	6	
7	7	
8	8	

MOTIVATION

GOAL ACHIEVE?		INFORMED ACCOUNTABILITY PARTNER		REWARD
Y	N	Y	N	

Notes:_______________________________________

____

____

____

DAILY ROUTINE

M	T	W	TH	F	S	SU

WAKE UP TIME:

DATE:

MEALS:
✓

GOALS	ROUTINES
1	1
2	2
3	3
4	4
5	5
6	6
7	7
8	8

B
L
D
S

MOTIVATION

GOAL ACHIEVE?	INFORMED ACCOUNTABILITY PARTNER	REWARD
Y N	Y N	

Notes:_______________________________

____

____

____

DAILY ROUTINE

M	T	W	TH	F	S	SU

WAKE UP TIME:

DATE:

GOALS	ROUTINES	MEALS: ✓
1	1	B
2	2	L
3	3	
4	4	D
5	5	
6	6	S
7	7	
8	8	

MOTIVATION

GOAL ACHIEVE?	INFORMED ACCOUNTABILITY PARTNER	REWARD
Y N	Y N	

Notes:_______________________________

____

____

____

9 798749 881233